For permissions, contact Tameka Echols.

Email: tamekalechols@gmail.com
Website: www.tamekaechols.com
Mailing: PO Box 210, Plano, IL 60545-0210

Printed in USA by Kairos Christian Publishing Co.

KEY STRATEGIES TO GET OUT OF "PIT"IFUL SITUATIONS

Author Tameka Echols

DEDICATION

I want to dedicate this book to my Savior and Lord, Jesus Christ for without Him, this assignment would not have been completed.

In addition, I would like to dedicate this book to my Christian Coach/Mentor - Sophia Ruffin-Wilson, founder of The Company of Copacetic Leaders™, and my teammates of this coaching and mentorship program for their prayers, encouragement, challenge, push, pull and help to birth the ability to write out of me that I didn't know existed.

Through prayer, fasting, and the leading of the Holy Spirit, her coaching helped me to come out of hiding, confront fear head-on, execute, and follow through with the completion of goals that I would never have completed without her guidance. To the future of writing, I go, in Jesus' Name!

ACKNOWLEDGMENTS

To my wonderful and loving husband, Quan.
I appreciate you for your endless prayers and
for supporting me in serving God
by serving others through ministry.
I honor you, sweetheart!

To my son, Kendall, and my daughter, Kaela
Your endless love and support in whatever
endeavor I set out to do is not unnoticed.

Many thanks to family, friends, and Christian
leaders for seeing something in me that I did
not see and loving me enough to help me
discover who I am in Christ. Thank you for
praying with me, for me, and for believing in
me when I didn't dare to believe in myself.

A special thanks to my amazing Publisher,
Linda D. Jernigan, M.A., and publishing team
for all of the late nights and early mornings
they sacrificed to help bring this book and my
previous book, *RISE UP & BE FREE* to
fruition.

Finally, I would like to acknowledge you, the
reader. Without your support, my efforts
would be fruitless. I am grateful for you!

TABLE OF CONTENTS

Dedication

Acknowledgements

Notes

About the Author

Contact

CHAPTER 1

HELP! I'M IN A PIT!

"I WAITED patiently for the Lord; and he inclined unto me, and heard my cry. He brought me up also out of an horrible pit, out of the miry clay, and set my feet upon a rock, and established my goings. And he hath put a new song in my mouth, even praise unto our God: many shall see it, and fear, and shall trust in the Lord"
(Psalm 40:1-3, KJV)

What do you do when everything seems to be going wrong? Where do you turn when life seems to be falling apart? Some people complain. Others get angry or maybe become overwhelmed with fear and depression. Conversely, there are those who get busy, attempting to get themselves out of the situation. However, what do you do when nothing seems to work, and you find yourself in a deep pit?

Easton's Bible Dictionary defines pit as: a hole in the ground (Exodus 21:33; Exodus 21:34), a cistern for water (Genesis 37:24; Jeremiah 14:3), a vault (Jeremiah 41:9), a grave (Psalm 30:3). It is used as a figure for mischief (Psalm 9:15), and is the name given to the unseen place of woe (Revelation 20:1; Revelation 20:3).

According to The New Strong's Expanded Exhaustive Concordance of the Bible, the word pit is used 88 times in Scripture passages. Pit is used 77 times in the Old Testament and 11 times in the New Testament (Strong et al., 2010).

Well, there are many instances where people find themselves in a pit. It could be a pit of emotional despair, financial hardship, mental anguish, physical pain, or something else. What's even more unfortunate is that many people get into the pit and never get out. Discouraged and defeated, they decide to remain where they are instead of determining to escape their pit and climb out.

I'm here to tell you that you can't afford to stay in the pit. Your life and your ultimate destiny depend on your determination to trust God and get out. A pit should never become a place of comfort.

The good news is that every pit has the potential to be temporary because the Word of God in the Bible promises that He will deliver us from every affliction. God's Word will never disappoint us! It says Isaiah 49:23 (NIV) that,

"Then you will know that I am the LORD;
those who hope in me
will not be disappointed."

CHAPTER 2

<u>I'M IN A PIT, NOW WHAT?</u>

A pit is a tough place to be in. A pit can differ in size depending on the size of your issue. This pit, defined in Chapter 1 as the "the unknown place of woe," can be a place of grief, misery, distress, and discomfort (Easton).

I have found myself in a pit or two throughout my years, and I can tell you, they are not a fun place to be!

In a pit, you can feel helpless, unsure, and alone. It can be a really dark place; where you know that there's nothing you can do for yourself and you understand that without some divine intervention, you are doomed!

Sometimes when you find yourself in a pit in life, it takes more than just the knowledge of who you are to get you out. Sometimes the only thing you can do is to just praise your way out. It's in the pit where you feel the least like praising Him, but praise in the pit is a praise that praises Him anyhow!

We can say thank you for anything and having a grateful heart is a great thing to have, but when we praise Him in the pit, we're not particularly praising Him for anything He's done, but just simply for who He is. It's that kind of praise that brings God right-smack-dab in the middle of that pit with you and when He comes *in*, you get lifted *out*!

In Psalm 22:23, David tells us that God inhabits the praises of His people. David knew a thing or two about pits and praising. To inhabit means that God fills that place.

In Acts Chapter 16, the Bible records the account of Paul and Silas when they had been severely beaten and thrown into the "*Pit of a prison*." They had every reason in the world to give up, but Paul looked over to Silas and said: "Hey brother Silas, let's praise Him!" Because of that praise, everything began to shake, similar to a natural earthquake, which caused things to shake, including the prison doors!

As a result, the prison doors were opened, and the shackles which held and bound them in that prison, fell completely off.

God caused an earthquake! He came to their rescue to get them out of prison. The earthquake was the effect of what happened when God came into the prison with them. God loves His children so much that He will go to great lengths and depths to rescue and free His people to bring them out of pits of darkness and place them in a victorious state of freedom because being in a PIT is not beyond God's power to deliver you from.

As a result of their prayers and praise, God got them out of their pit. God's people are so precious to Him that He said to His followers,

"I will never leave thee nor forsake thee"
Deuteronomy 31:8 (KJV)

Psalm 139:7-12 paints vivid pictures of how He will be with you always:

"Whither shall I go from thy spirit? or whither shall I flee from thy presence? If I ascend up into heaven, thou art there: if I make my bed in hell, behold, thou art there. If I take the wings of the morning, and dwell in the uttermost parts of the sea; Even there shall thy hand lead me, and thy right hand shall hold me.

If I say, Surely the darkness shall cover me;
even the night shall be light about me. Yea,
the darkness hideth not from thee; but the
night shineth as the day: the darkness and
the light are both alike to thee."

Matthew 28:20 (KJV) informs God's people of this promise,

"...I am with you always, even unto the end
of the world. Amen"

These scriptures confirms and reinforce that even in "Pit"iful situations, God is with you!

CHAPTER 3

I'M IN A PIT?

Someone may be asking the question; how do people get in a pit? Well, here are three ways that a person can get into a pit. First, you can be thrown into a pit. Second, you can slip or fall into a pit, and third, you can jump into a pit. For example, in the Bible, there were several characters that experienced a pit situation.

Joseph was thrown into a pit (Genesis 37:24) The prophet Jeremiah was thrown into a pit (Jeremiah Chapter 38:9), David fell into a pit of despair as a result of unwise decisions (Psalm 7:15; Psalm 40:2), and the prodigal son jumped into a pit of reckless choices (Luke 15:11-17).

Just like these men, in one point of my life, I found myself in a pit. I fell into a deep pit of depression.

Over 30 years ago, I made a decision that I was going to end my life. I was under a heavy level of stress, anxiety, and pressure. I felt that I had no reason to live anymore.

I somehow believed in my mind that I was only a burden to my family. I presumed that no one would ever want to date me, marry me, love me and that no one would care if I was dead or alive. I felt like a misfit and didn't seem to fit in anywhere or with any particular group of people. All my thoughts were negative, and I began to speak negatively. I felt helpless, hopeless, and worthless.

One day, I stood in the bathroom of my parent's home with tears streaming down my face and a razor blade in my left hand ready to end it all. At a point of anguish, I cried out, "Jesus!" "Help me!" "Save me!"

I fell to my knees and told Him that I didn't want to do this. I said to Him that I want to live and not die. I just wanted the pains of life to go away.

In that moment, I felt the love of Jesus wrap His arms around me and He told me everything was going to be okay. I felt a comfort and a peace that I had never experienced before.

I began to think how sad, hurt, and disappointed my family and friends would be to know that I was no longer here. I knew then that going that route was not an option and that things would get better.

Well, things did get better. Because God chose me in Him before the foundation of the Earth and has a unique plan for my life, I graduated high school with honors. I married my high school sweetheart, was blessed with two beautiful children. I developed a successful career in banking and healthcare, established an award-winning catering business, graduated from college - cum laude (with honors), and was selected as a university Ambassador for the school's online campus community.

I have humbly served as a servant for Christ in seven global ministries in multiple roles in three states. I've been acknowledged as a best-selling author, interviewed on a Stellar Gospel Music Award winning morning radio show, was featured in three magazines, presented on over 250 national platforms including ABC, CBS, NBC, USA Today, and FOX, and now listed among the history books in the Library of Congress research library in Washington, D.C.

By the grace of God, I have emerged in leadership as a mentor and advocate for a Christian mentoring program and was later licensed and ordained as an evangelist and a pastor. Also, I earned over 100 Certificates of Completion in healthcare, chosen to be a primary facilitator alongside my husband to lead a Discipleship 101 New Members Class, and, recently earned a Certificate of Teaching as a Christian educator.

As I reflect on my life, to think that the whispers of Satan tried to drown out the voice of God and bury me in a pit darkness with no chance of seeing the light of day again. To think how he injected negative thoughts to steal my peace, my joy, and attempt to destroy my life.

To think how the enemy tried to abort my destiny but I decided to turn from the darkness of Satan's voice and all of the negative things he was speaking and turn towards the Light of Jesus and loving voice of my Father.

As a living witness of the goodness of

God, I can say that Satan's plans will NOT prevail over God's people! His plans will NOT thwart God's plan for our lives! Satan's schemes and plots will NOT succeed!

Satan is our vicious enemy, but he will NOT be victorious in my life or your life! Jesus' victory gives us victory over the evil one! Jesus came so that we might have life and have it more abundantly (John 10:10).

When you feel like giving up, want to quit, or throw in the towel, count the cost and be reminded that God loves you and has not forgotten about you.

God will not give up on you! He wants you to live and have a beautiful and blessed life because His plan for your life is amazing! You have a purpose and **YOUR LIFE MATTERS**!

JESUS is the only way to a better life

and is the only One to help you rise up from a "pit"iful place in life, be delivered, healed, be set free, and experience the joy of the Lord in extraordinary ways!

As you can see, like the men of the Bible I mentioned earlier in this chapter, Jesus intervened and reached out and rescued me from a pit of depression, restored my soul, filled me with joy, and transformed the course of my life for His glory.

We have a deliverer, and His name is Jesus. He is the only One to provide hope to the hopeless. There is no pit too deep, no fall, slip, or jump too low for God to not deliver you from. Pit life is not God's best for you and He never intended for you to get into it, settle in it, stay in it, nor get comfortable in it!

A pit is not the dwelling place that God has for you. You must decide a pit is not a normal way to live nor is it your permanent residence! As a son or daughter of God, you were created to live at palace level and not pit level.

He is patiently waiting for you to turn to Him and call on Him in faith so He can answer and rescue you from "pit"iful situations!

Here are some sure ways to tell if you are in a pit. You know you're in a pit when you feel stuck. Another way to tell is that you don't feel like getting up or out; and lastly when you've lost your vision.

These three key signs are powerful because if you get so caught up in what's going on around you, you can become lost and feel hopeless about the future. However, here's the good news! Hopelessness and feeling helpless are not permanent feelings.

You must believe that things will get better and that there is a way to get out of a pit and regain hope. Jesus Christ is your way up and your way out!

Also, you may need to call on family members, friends, or join a support group. You may even consider contacting a leader at a local church or look for a mentor, a coach, or seek professional secular and Christian counseling to help shine a light of hope on your life's journey towards a better future.

"For if they fall, the one will lift up his fellow: but woe to him that is alone when he falleth; for he hath not another to help him up."
Ecclesiastes 4:10 (KJV)

Another example can be to write out an action plan that will lead towards a positive outcome of getting out of "pit"iful situations. You could start by asking yourself some questions:

1. What can I do today to help me get out of this pit?

2. What can I do this week to help me get out of this pit?

3. What can I do this month to help me get out of this pit?

4. What are some things that I believe are hindering me from getting out of this pit?

5. What do I visualize my life looking like once I get out of this pit?

You must make a decision to take the necessary steps needed to get out and stay out!

God said He sees our future. He sees the light at the end of a dark tunnel. When we think all hope is gone, God can bring us out of the pit. God says,

"Commit your future to the LORD! Trust in him, and he will act on your behalf"
Psalm 37:5, (NET).

The Word of God informs us,

"And the LORD answered me and said, Write the vision and make it plain upon tables, that he may run that readeth it"
Habakkuk 2:2 (KJV).

The Lord said to write the vision and make it plain because you can only run with the information you have close to your heart!

Being thrown into a pit can be an awful experience. It can come from out of nowhere. You could be going along minding your own business and suddenly, you look around and you are in a place that you have no idea how you got there. This pit is known as a "pit of innocence."

You were thrown in without having anything to do with it. One of the first pit situations occurred in Genesis where Joseph's brothers threw him into a pit. The Word says, "And they took him and cast him into a pit: and the pit was empty, there was no water in it."

Have you ever been thrown into a pit of innocence? Maybe it was someone's jealousy or insecurity about you. Maybe it was someone else's act of selfishness or greed. Sometimes it could just be that you were in the wrong place at the wrong time. As we can see, people can put us into a pit.

Life is full of challenges and no one is immune to the impact that these challenges will have on your life. Regardless of age, gender, race, religion or even social and economic status, troubling times will come. While some people suffer in silence, few will talk about it in hopes of getting free from a pit themselves or to help someone else to get out of a pit.

Sometimes, a pit situation can be the trigger of a mental health event that causes a traumatic experience. This is something that happened to me. When I was 19, I landed my dream job! Something about being a bank teller appealed to me since I was a kid and when given the opportunity, I felt such joy and happiness!

On my one-month anniversary at the job, the branch where I worked was robbed and I experienced a horrifying crime of being robbed at gun point! The roller coaster of emotions I felt would haunt me for many years.

The perpetrator was armed and showed little concern as he went about his act. See, I was pregnant at the time, but it didn't stop him from firing his gun at me...twice! Imagine you are working your dream job, pregnant with your first child, your emotions are all over the place and then something happens that puts everything in your life in jeopardy.

For years, I suffered in silence. I couldn't fully express what I was feeling to my family or friends. It was determined after many doctors' visits that I suffered from post-traumatic stress disorder, major depression, and would often have excessive anxiety.

Panic attacks, flashbacks, and depression always surrounded me. I didn't feel safe anywhere and I was nervous everywhere I went. You see, someone dealing with mental health issues can have symptoms that present themselves in many ways; from insomnia to extreme fatigue, eating disorders, overwhelming fear; along with nightmares, and hallucinations to name a few. There is no real hard and fast rule to what one might go through but one thing common to all mental health issues is that the effects of it can be devastating.

My trigger was a criminal who decided to take what wasn't his, violently. Someone who, even after getting what he came to take, shot at a pregnant woman. While I wasn't hit (praise God) I did suffer a traumatic brain injury when I hit my head on the open safe door in my workstation under the teller station as I fell to the ground to protect myself and unborn child from the flying bullets.

Let me tell you, trauma can cause an indescribable feeling of helpless and hopelessness. For me, I didn't realize how disconnected from everything I was and how much this affected me physically, mentally, and emotionally and how deep in a pit of despair I was in until I received counseling. It was a terrible time in my life. It took a long time for me to build up the courage to start going outside and doing things without feeling paranoid or constantly looking over my shoulder feeling like something else was going to happen to me or my baby. I thought that I would never get out of this "pit"iful situation of mental anguish.

It took over 10 years before I could even drive near the bank where the incident occurred. The crazy thing out of all of this was the enemy tried to destroy my son and I, but God stepped in and said, "NO!"

My story could have ended tragically but God saw it another way! See, those bullets did not hit me. After the incident, I did not quit the company that I worked for. God healed me and blessed me with an office position at another location which allowed me to establish a wonderful career in banking that spanned over 20 years. What the enemy meant for evil; God turned it for my good!

I give praise to God because He is the Father of compassion and all comfort. He is a healer and a deliverer!

It took time for me to forgive this person and to my knowledge, was never caught for the crime. God touched my heart so that I could feel again. God was able to soften my heart and I committed to the process of forgiving, healing through His love, compassion, grace and tender mercies.

See, unforgiveness did not affect the robber, it just kept me bound and stuck in a pit. I had to hand over the prison key that was keeping me captive so that I could experience freedom and fulfill God's purpose in my life. Psalm 57:2 (ESV) says,

"I cry out to God Most High, to God who fulfills his purpose for me."

Maybe you might be dealing with something, and you are finding it difficult to forgive someone for what they did to you or you have a hard time trusting people. Take some time (as much as you need) to get in the presence of the Lord and allow the Holy Spirit to heal your heart so that you can fully experience love, joy, trust, and peace which surpasses all understanding.

God has the perfect prescription and plan for you to live a healthy life, which may include speaking to someone through secular therapy, Christian counseling, and receiving pastoral counseling to help lift you out of "pit'iful situations.

These are promises for good days and for dark ones, too.

"Draw near to God,
and he will draw near to you"
James 4:8 (NKJV)

"The LORD is near to the brokenhearted
and saves the crushed in spirit"
Psalm 34:18 (ESV).

"For with God nothing shall be impossible"
Luke 1:37 (KJV)

The next way you can get into a pit is to slip in. Unlike the pit where we were thrown in, this one we managed somehow to get into ourselves. We don't know how it happened. We can say that we got distracted, we weren't paying attention, and everything seemed fine. We thought everything was going well, then suddenly whoops, you've slipped right into the pit!

You didn't plan this or ever wanted this to happen. The thought of slipping never even crossed your mind. You had no idea that this was how things would turn out. You didn't even see it coming. Now you realize that you've gotten yourself into something deep. You've slipped and messed up. You've fallen and can't get up. Now, what do you do? You can call out to the Lord to save you and help you.

Psalm 40:12-13 (NIV) says,

"For troubles without number surround me; my sins have overtaken me, and I cannot see. They are more than the hairs on my head, and my heart fails within me. Be pleased, O Lord, to save me; O Lord, come quickly to help me."

The last way you can get into a pit is to jump in. Maybe you got angry, or were bitter about something, became frustrated, was hurt, or disappointed. Sometimes our foolishness can cause us to jump into a pit.

You know what you were about to do was wrong. You had time to consider it and think about the consequences for your actions and you really didn't want to do it, but you went ahead and did exactly what you didn't want to, knowing that the outcome would result in something negative. You enjoyed the trip that sin took you on, but you didn't enjoy the costs of the fare you paid when you jumped into a pit of sin.

Romans 7:15 (AMP) puts it this way,

"For I do not understand my own actions [I am baffled and bewildered by them.] I do not practice what I want to do, but I am doing the very thing I hate [and yielding to

my human nature, my worldliness – my
sinful capacity.]"

In Job 33 verse 28 it says that God wants you to turn back your soul from the pit so that the light of life may shine on you. Now, who wouldn't want the light of the Lord to shine on them? It's time to start yielding to God's warnings before we even get close to a pit!

CHAPTER 4

HOW TO GET OUT OF A PIT

Now that you know some ways that you can get into a pit. We need to find out how we can get out of a pit.

There are three steps that you can take to get out of your pit.

- ❖ Step one – CRY OUT
- ❖ Step two – CONFESS
- ❖ Step three –CONSENT

I must say that before you can even take a single step to get out of the pit, you must admit that you're in a pit!

According to The Project Gutenberg eBook of Webster's Unabridged Dictionary, the word admit is defined as: "To suffer to enter; to grant entrance, whether into a place, or into the mind, or consideration; to receive;

to take; as, they were into his house; to admit a serious thought into the mind; To concede as true; to acknowledge or assent to, as an allegation which it is impossible to deny; to own or confess; as, the argument or fact is admitted; he admitted his guilt" (Various & Lawrence, 2009).

By admitting or acknowledging that you are in a pit helps you to be honest with yourself, become aware, put things into perspective, and recognize that you are faced with something that's bigger than you and you need some help to get up and get out. You can't break free from a pit until you admit that you are in one. After your admission, the first thing you do is cry out.

You might be wondering, what does it mean to cry out to God? Well, I'm so glad that you asked! Crying out to God has nothing to do with tears. Tears are great but crying out to God is much more than tears.

Often tears fall because of the pain of the consequences of our decisions or the negative decisions of others. We aren't crying out to God; we are crying to God about what happened. That's a big difference!

Crying out to God implies something much deeper – something from the depths of your soul. It could be crying out to God with joy, excitement, and enthusiasm. Or it could be crying out to God in pain, or anguish, or despair. Crying out just means going deep inside your soul and calling out to God from that place.

This takes us back to Psalm 40:1 where David said,

"I waited patiently for the Lord: he turned to me and heard my cry." David also said in Psalm 3:4 that, *"He cried unto the Lord with his voice and he heard me out of his holy hill. Selah."*

I believe that God waits for the cry of His children to remove all doubt as to who came to the rescue. He wants to deliver us from the pits of life, but we must cry out to Him from our soul as if our life depended on it.

When we cry out to God, we are sending the petition of our hearts straight up to the throne of God! God is sovereign. He is the One who made all things, rules all things, and can change all things in our lives if we believe. Only God can bring us out of a pit!

When was the last time you cried out to God or spent time lamenting before the Lord? I am not asking when was the last time was you prayed. I'm saying when was the last time you truly cried out to God from the depth of your heart – expressing whatever emotion or feeling is in there?

In the New International Version of the Bible, the Lord said in Exodus 3:7-8 that,

"I have indeed seen the misery of my people in Egypt. I have heard them crying out because of their slave drivers, and I am concerned about their suffering. So, I have come down to rescue them from the hand of the Egyptians and to bring them up out of that land into a good and spacious land, a land flowing with milk and honey…"

If the Lord heard the people of Egypt cry out, why wouldn't you think He would do the same for you? He is the same yesterday, today, and forever! Because He is the same yesterday, I know that what He has said remains true for you and me today.

David told us in Psalm 72:12 (NIV),

"For he will deliver the needy who cry out, the afflicted who have no one to help."
The second step to get out of the pit is to confess. After you cry out to God, confess.

The Word says in I John 1:9 (KJV) that,

"If we confess our sins, he is faithful and just to forgive us our sins, and to cleanse us from all unrighteousness."

Take time to tell the Lord what kind of mess you got yourself into. Talk to Him about what you think is holding you back and keeping you in the pit. Tell Him what you are feeling in your heart. Let His light shine on you so He can heal you. Don't let pride get in the way of confessing to God. Pride is one of the biggest sins that can keep you in the pit longer than you want to!

Bear your heart and soul before God. Talk to Him about things that you have done, problems that you are facing, and things that made you mad or hurt. Repent and ask God to forgive you and tell Him how much you need Him.

The Word says in Psalm 145:18 (NIV) that,

"The Lord is near to all who call on him, to all who call on him in truth."

After we (1) cry out to God and (2) make our confessions to Him, we will need to consent. According to the Merriam-Webster Collegiate Dictionary, the definition of consent is, "Compliance in or approval of what is done or proposed by another…agreement as to action or opinion…voluntary agreement."

Consenting means saying "YES" to God and whatever it is that He commands you to do – regardless of what "*IT*" may be.

You've tried time and time again to get yourself out of the pit but now it is time to allow God to do it His way. What is His way you might ask? I can't tell you exactly what His way is but I'll tell you this about His way…**IT ISN'T LIKE YOUR WAY**!

The Word says in Isaiah 55:8-9 (NKJV),

"For My thoughts are not your thoughts, nor are your ways My ways," says the Lord. "For as the heavens are higher than the earth, so are My ways higher than your ways, And My thoughts than your thoughts."

I don't know what God will ask you to do to get out of your pit. He may ask you to leave a relationship. He may ask you to apologize. He may ask you to forgive. He may ask you to change some habits. I don't know. But I do know this one thing, *"**HIS WAY IS BETTER THAN YOUR WAY!**"*

The question is, are you willing to accept that? Can you accept it mentally and truly internalize the concept that God's way is better than your way? If not, you might want to hold off on packing up to get out of the pit.

Your time in the pit might not be done.

Listen, every child of God must experience some "pits." We must go through some things, in order for God to use us! I've discovered that any area of life where I am NOT consenting to God's will – whether relational, financial, emotional, spiritual, or whatever – is an area where I am almost guaranteed to end up in a pit. Any area where you don't consent to God's way is an area where you'll be in a pit.

It is important for us to understand that consent is an exciting part of the process of getting out of the pit. Consent involves receiving God's blessing to get out of the pit. It is God's will for you to get out of that pit!

You can have confidence and reassurance that while you are waiting on God to get you out of that pit, He is working behind the scenes on your behalf! He is shifting and rearranging things to get you out of that pit!

When you actively consent to the Lord, turn everything over to Him so He can work it out.

The Word says in I John 5:14-15 (NIV),

"This is the confidence we have in approaching God: that if we ask anything according to his will, he hears us. And if we know that he hears us—whatever we ask—we know that we have what we asked of him."

So, cry out, confess, and consent to the will of God, and remember that faith cometh by hearing, and hearing by the word of God. God's way miraculously leads to deliverance, freedom, and victory!

CHAPTER 5

HOW TO STAY OUT OF A PIT

Now that you have read about different ways to get into "Pit"iful situations and how to get out of them, there are some key questions that you can ask yourself to help you stay out. Ask yourself the following questions and be honest:

- ❖ Am I surrendering my will to God?
- ❖ Am I sending my worries to God?
- ❖ Am I strengthening my walk with God?
- ❖ Am I seeing the work of God?

If the answer to any of these questions is no, then I would suggest that you come to Him today in prayer and get that area of your life straightened out. There is peace in Jesus. There is power in Jesus. You can get your life out of the pit if you will do it God's way!

I don't know anything about you or your life, but I do know this. You weren't meant to live in a pit. If you recall, a pit can be recognized as a grave or even hell. Only dead people and dead things remain in deep, dark, and demised places!

As long as you have breath in your body, have a will to live, hope for a better future, and faith in God, you can draw strength from Him, receive peace in your heart and mind, and gain confidence in knowing that God will save you and come to your rescue and pull you out of "pit"iful situations!

The time to get out is right now! Why stay any longer? It's time to get out and start living life like it was meant to be. You have to say to yourself over and over again that I will no longer dwell in the pit. Cry out to God today.

Confess and bare your soul before God today and consent to His plan today. If you are willing to do those three things, then let me be the first to congratulate you and say that you are well on your way out of the pit!

It's time to get excited about what's to come because what's to come is better than what's been! Your future is waiting on you and it's time to rejoice and be glad about what the Lord is going to do in your life.

Start to thank Him and praise Him even while you are waiting for Him to pull you out! Make up your mind to trust in God, get a new song in your mouth and heart, and sing a hymn of praise to our God. Wave goodbye, say so long, and farewell to your "pit"ful situations for the Lord is at hand!

Keep looking up and you will get out! God will bless you, make His face shine upon you, and give you peace as you climb out of "pit"iful situations!

Now, I want you to take a deep breath in and out, hold your head up, stretch your arms out wide, smile, and live in freedom to:

- *Believe again*
- *Breathe again*
- *Dance again*
- *Dream again*
- *Experience joy again*
- *Fast again*
- *Hope again*
- *Have faith again*
- *Have peace again*
- *Laugh again*
- *Lift your hands again*
- *Live again*
- *Love again*
- *Pray again*
- *Praise again*
- *See again*
- *Shout again*
- *Smile again*

Worship again and rise up, again because
God is with you and will bring you out!

CHAPTER 6

PRAYER OF SALVATION

God loves you and as a human being, one of the most important relationships that you can have is having a personal relationship with Jesus Christ.

If you desire to experience a one-of-a-kind, life-long relationship that you have never known, take a moment to pray this prayer below to invite Jesus into your heart and receive Him as your Savior and Lord:

Lord Jesus,
I admit that I am a sinner and I need your
forgiveness and I repent of my sins. I confess
with my mouth the Lord Jesus and believe in
my heart that God raised Jesus from the
dead, and I will be saved. Jesus, I accept
you as my personal Savior and invite you to
be the Lord of my life.

Jesus, come into my heart and fill me with the Holy Spirit. Lead me and help me to be the person that you want me to be. Thank You for loving me and saving me and now that I am saved, I will live with You in eternity, forever. In Jesus name, Amen.

Welcome to God's Family
and your new life in Christ!

CHAPTER 7

OUT OF THE PIT PRAYER

Heavenly Father,
thank you for loving me, leading,
guiding, and directing me. You are such a
good, good Father and care about
everything that concerns me.

Thank you, Lord, that no matter what
situation, circumstance, or "pit" that I may
find myself in, I can trust and believe that
you will be right there with me and will
bring me out when I call on you. Father,
You said in Psalm 17:6 that when I call on
You, You will answer.

So in the Name of Jesus, I ask for You to
heal me, deliver me, and set me free from
pits of: abuse, addiction, anger, anxiety,
betrayal, bitterness, confusion, deception,
depression, despair, disappointment,
double-mindedness, envy, embarrassment,

*fear, failure, greed, grief, guilt, hate, hurt,
insecurity, illness, imperfection, inadequacy,
intimidation, isolation, jealousy, lack,
laziness, lying, manipulation, moodiness,
non-confidence, negativity, offense,
oppression, pain, perversion, pride, poverty,
profanity, quarreling, rebellion, rejection,
regret, retaliation, resentment, sadness,
shame, stubbornness, temptation, trauma,
temper, unforgiveness, violence, weariness,
weakness, and worry.*

*Father, thank you for delivering, healing,
and setting me free today. Thank you for the
great things that you are going to do in my
life now that I am out of the pit! I give Your
name the glory, honor, and praise because
victory today is mine! In Jesus' name, I pray,
Amen!*

NOTES

Easton, M. G. (n.d.). *Pit - Easton's Bible dictionary online*. Bible Study Tools. https://www.biblestudytools.com/dictionaries/eastons-bible-dictionary/pit.html

M.G. Easton M.A., D.D., Illustrated Bible Dictionary, Third Edition, published by Thomas Nelson, 1897. Public Domain, copy freely.

Merritt, J. (n.d.). How to Get Your Life out of the Pit. Retrieved from http://www.sermonnotebook.org/new testament/1 Pet 5_5-10.htm

Moore, B. (2007). Get Out of That Pit. Nashville, CA: Thomas Nelson, Inc.

Official King James Bible Online. King James Bible Online. (n.d.). https://www.kingjamesbibleonline.org

Strong, J., Vine, W. E., & Kohlenberger, J. R. (2010). Main Concordance - Pit. In *The New Strong's Expanded Exhaustive Concordance of the Bible* (Red Letter, p. 667). essay, T. Nelson.

StudyDesk - General Bible Search - Woe. StudyLight.org. (n.d.). https://www.studylight.org/study-desk.html?q1=Woe&OLWordSearchRange=beg&q2=&ss=0&t1=eng_kjv&t2=eng_kjv&t3=eng_nas&ns=0&sr=1&ot=bhs&nt=na26&b=chapter&d=3

Various, & Lawrence, G. (2009, August 22). Admit. The Project Gutenberg eBook of Webster's Unabridged Dictionary. https://www.gutenberg.org/cache/epub/29765/pg29765-images.html#chap01

Scripture references were taken from the Holy Bible, New International Version, and New King James Version.

ABOUT THE AUTHOR

Tameka Echols is an esteemed wife, mother, pastor, evangelist, intercessor, author, mentor, speaker, and teacher with a heart to win lost souls. Tameka has a passion to serve God, the church, and the community by reaching out with a hand and heart of compassion to be salt and light in the word and spread the love and joy of Jesus Christ to others.

Her life is dedicated to living by the example of following Christ and encouraging men and women on how to live up to their full potential in Him. Her decision to follow Christ has led her to develop, grow, receive deliverance in Christ, be discipled, and strengthened in her faith in Christ; which has led her to discover and experience her God ordained destiny.

Tameka believes it is because she gives of herself selflessly to others that she is providing service to God Himself. It is He who gave her gifts and abilities as a faithful steward of His grace in order to serve in unique multifaceted capacities. Tameka is a licensed minister of the Gospel, best-selling author, and holds an Associate degree and Bachelor's degree in Paralegal Studies. She's been married over 30 years and has two kingdom-purposed children.

CONTACT PAGE

Key Strategies to Get Out of "Pit"iful Situations
Author, Mrs. Tameka Echols

Website:
www.tamekalechols.com

Email:
tamekalechols@gmail.com

Mailing:
PO Box 210
Plano, IL 60545-0210

~Additional eBooks by Author Tameka Echols~

- *RISE UP & BE FREE*

- *LESSONS FROM COVID 19 2020 – 26 STORIES, ONE PANDEMIC*

Available on www.tamekaechols.com